Board Games

by
Harriot Blanchard

Illustrated by
Damon Burnard

TOYS AND GAMES

Books in this series

Action Toys
Board Games
Models
Puppets

Editor: Cally Chambers
Design: Kudos Design Services

First published in 1991 by
Wayland (Publishers) Ltd
61 Western Road, Hove
East Sussex, BN3 1JD, England

Typeset by Kudos Editorial and Design Services, Sussex, England
Printed in Italy by G.Canale & C.S.p.A.
Bound in France by A.G.M.

British Library Cataloguing in Publication Data
Blanchard, Harriot
    Board games. - (Toys and games)
    I. Title II. Series
    793

ISBN 0-7502-0099-5

Contents

Clean Up!

This is a game for just one player.

You are in charge of three street sweepers in a town covered with litter.

Your aim is to clean up all the litter before the sweepers go home for tea.

You play with fourteen cards.

Three of these have a sweeper and the number 6 on one side. On the back is a cup of tea.

The rest of the cards show shops surrounded by rubbish.
They are numbered: 1 2 3 4 5 (not 6) 7 8 9 10 11.

The backs show the same shops when the litter has been swept up.

Arrange all the cards to form a street,
number side up, in any order you like.

Use two dice to play.

The dice scores can
be used separately
or added together.

So, if you throw a 7 and a
3 you can either turn both
those cards over, or add
the numbers together and
turn over card 10.

If you throw a 6 you must
turn over a sweeper to
show he has gone home
for tea.

Can you clean up the
street before all the
sweepers go home
for tea?

How Clean Up! works

To win at *Clean Up!* you have to be lucky with the dice, even though you do have some control over how you use the dice scores.

To clean up before the sweepers go home, you must throw all the other numbers before three throws of 6 come up.

This kind of chance game is based on probability. You can change the probability that you will win by changing the cards.

If you have five sweepers you will be more likely to win. But with only two, you would have to be very lucky to clean up the rubbish before the sweepers went for tea.

Try this out for yourself, but remember – it's all down to chance in the end!

Driving Home

You can invent other games that use probability.
Here's one for you to try.

The goal of this game is to drive home before your car runs out of petrol.

The board opposite shows the controls of a car and a road made up of 60 spaces, numbered 1-60.

At the start of the game the petrol gauge shows full.
The gauge has 3 cards to take away, each numbered 6. Underneath it reads 'empty'.

Start with a counter or little car on square 1. Roll two dice, add the score and drive away. If you roll a 6, you must remove one petrol card from the gauge and not move around the board.

Will your luck hold and get you home before your petrol tank empties?

You can alter the probability of this game by including some petrol station squares.
Landing on these would allow you to refill your tank.

What game would you invent using the idea of a horse race?

7

Lotto

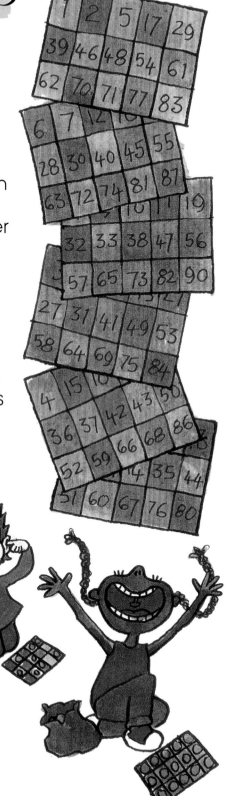

Lotto, or *Bingo*, is a game for 2 to 6 players.

The first player to collect a set of fifteen numbers is the winner.

There are six *Lotto* sheets, each marked with fifteen numbers between 1 and 90.
None of the numbers are repeated on other cards.

There are 90 numbered discs in a bag.

Without looking into the bag, the players take it in turn to pull out a disc.

The number is called out and the disc goes to the player with that number on his or her sheet. The disc covers the number.

You could be lucky enough to pull out one of the numbers on your own card.

The winner is the first to cover all the numbers on his or her sheet.

There are different types of *Lotto*, but you always need luck to be the first to collect and cover all the numbers on your *Lotto* sheet.

You could invent games like *Lotto*, in which you have to collect pictures instead of numbers.

The pictures could build a house, fill a farmyard with animals or rob a tomb to make *Frankenstein's Monster* (see next page).

9

Frankenstein's Monster

This game is like *Lotto*, but pictures are used instead of numbers.

Turn a shoe box into a tomb. Make sure it opens.

You will need to cut out 42 cards, all of the same size. On these draw and colour in:

- 6 heads
- 6 pairs of feet
- 6 bodies
- 12 arms (6 right and 6 left)
- 12 legs (6 right and 6 left)

Put all the cards in the tomb. The youngest player goes first and, in turn, the tomb is passed around.

When it's your turn, without looking, take a card.

If you pull out a part of the body that you've already got, you must put it back and that turn is wasted.

The goal is to be the first to complete a *Frankenstein's Monster*.

Each time you play you create a new monster, because the cards you pick will be different.

Here is an idea for another game in which the players collect a set of pieces.

The difference is they must be collected in a special order:

1 foundations
2 walls
3 rest of the house in any order.

Try making this game work with Lego pieces.

11

The Royal Game of Ur

The oldest known board game was discovered in the Royal Tombs of Ur. It was played in Iraq from about 5,000 years ago.

No one can work out how the game was played. But a clue might lie with the casting sticks that were found with it.

They were dark ebony on one side and light ivory on the other.

By throwing the sticks and then counting the number of light or dark sides showing, they controlled the game like simple dice.

Ten lion pieces and ten jackal pieces were also found in the tomb.

This is what the game's board looked like.

Historians are still trying to work out the rules. Their best guess is that it was some kind of race game.
Can you think of ways it could be played?

Junk Shop Game

Hidden away in a junk shop you find this board.

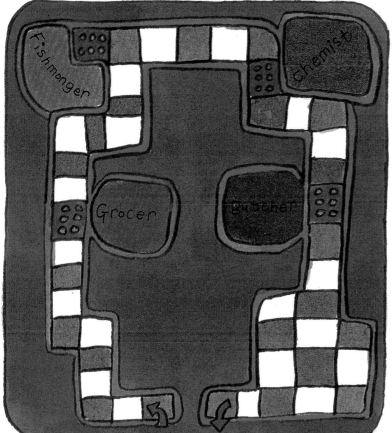

Next to it, in an old tin, you find models of:

- 4 little people
- 4 fish
- 4 little medicine bottles
- 4 apples
- 4 sausages
- some ice lolly sticks with jokes on one side.

But you can't find any rules.

The shopkeeper sells the game to you for only ten pence, because nobody knows how to play it.

Can you work out your own game?
Design a board and the pieces, and make up the rules.
Then challenge a friend to work out how it is played.

Ludo or Pachisi

Ludo is a race game that first appeared in Britain in 1896. The Victorians got the idea for *Ludo* from an Indian game called *Pachisi*.

Instead of dice, the Indians used six cowrie shells. They threw the shells and worked out the score by counting the numbers of mouths facing up.

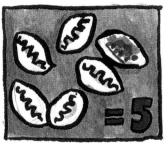

One mouth up scored 10, any other number facing up scored that number of points and none at all scored 25. *Pachisi* means 'twenty-five'.

The board for *Pachisi* was usually made out of cloth and was shaped like a cross.

14

The North Indian emperors loved *Pachisi* so much that it amused them to dress up sixteen slaves in four team colours to act as counters.

The red and white paving stones in the palace courtyards of Agra and Allahabad were used as boards.

Nowadays, *Ludo* is played with a square board and coloured counters.

The Aztecs in Peru had their own version of *Ludo*. They called it *Patolli*.

Obviously the idea behind the game has always been popular. One reason may be that it is so simple.

In both *Pachisi* and *Ludo,* the winner is the first player to get their four counters home.

Animal Ludo

This game uses a *Ludo* board, a die and a shaker. But instead of four sets of coloured counters, as you would find in a traditional version of *Ludo*, each player has a type of animal.

Player 1 has eight ants. Because there are so many of them they have 2 throws every turn.

Player 2 has two slow snails in the race. They only move when they shake 1, 4 or 6.

Player 3 has two scampering mice. They have to go around the board twice before they can go home.

And player 4 is a blackbird which has to fly round four times before going home.

Which of these animals do you think has the best chance of winning? You can make the pieces and use a *Ludo* board to play.

16

The Maze Game

Ludo uses just the die to control the game. But you can make a more exciting race game with two decision makers:

- a die to control the distance you move

- and a spinner to control the direction.

Draw out a board like this:

Rescue

Prisoner

?

Use spinner for direction of next move.

Dead end. Lose prisoner and return to start.

Your goal is to land on a 'rescue' square, pick up a prisoner and get out. If you land on a '?' you must use the spinner to find out the direction of your next move.
A green square leads you into a dead end; you go back to the start and your prisoner returns to prison.

17

Race Games in History

In race games through history, the aim has always been for players to move around a marked course. Only the boards vary in the way they have been drawn and the story that they tell.

The hundreds of race games invented in the last four centuries often come from one called *The Game of the Goose*. A version of this may have been played by the ancient Greeks, but Franciso dei Medici (1541 – 87) of Italy first made it popular all over Europe in the sixteenth century.

From the eighteenth century on, both the French and the British liked to invent board games that helped children to learn all sorts of subjects.

This game, called *The Circle of Knowledge. A New Game of the Wonders of Nature, Science and Art*, was made around 1845. It is quite like the modern knowledge game, *Trivial Pursuit*.

It is interesting to look at old board games in books and museums, because they often show popular pastimes or events of their time and how people behaved.

The Victorians took the race game of *Snakes and Ladders* from an Indian one called *Muksha-patamu*, which was a religious game about good and evil. In *Snakes and Ladders*, if you were good you moved up a ladder, but being naughty sent you down a snake.

The Victorians especially enjoyed race games that told a story. In *Office Boy*, the story was about starting work in the bottom job and working up to be the boss.

The track had spaces marked 'hard-working', 'careful' and 'honest'. If you landed on one of these you got an extra go. Other spaces were marked 'cheat', 'lazy' and 'careless'. If you landed on these you missed a turn.

TV Star

This game is about some children who really want to be on TV. They daydream about becoming TV stars.

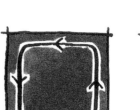

On scrap paper, work out designs for a track with a Start and a Finish. Here are some ideas.

The track could be from 50 to 100 spaces long. When you are happy with your design, draw it carefully on card.

Along the length of the track, mark 10 'Risk!' squares. As you play the game, landing on Risk! squares means that you must pick up a Risk! card. This could be good or bad news. You will need to make 10 small cards, each 10 by 5 cm. Write half of the cards with good news and half with bad. Here are some examples of good news:

- your uncle makes TV programmes (take an extra turn)
- your letter is picked out to be read on *Blue Peter* (go forward 7 squares)

and bad news:

- you catch measles (miss 2 turns)
- you forget to put a stamp on your letter to *Blue Peter* (start again)

When you have thought of other news for your Risk! cards, you can go ahead and play.

You need 2 to 4 players, and a die and shaker with your board. Make sure the Risk! cards are shuffled and face down. The youngest player goes first.

You can make your own race game that follows a story.

Start by thinking of a good story which has a goal, like reaching the moon or topping the charts.

21

Goats and Gardeners

A gardener has fifteen beautiful flowers. Three hungry goats have strayed into her garden.

When the game starts, the board is empty. One player places flowers, the other moves the goats.

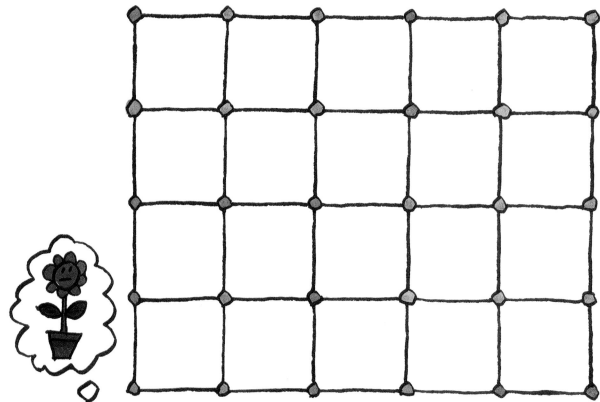

The players take it in turns to position their pieces on any empty point. Two pieces cannot be on the same point.

Pieces can only move around the board when they have all been placed. Then flowers go first and after they have had three turns, the goats can move.

This is how the flowers move:

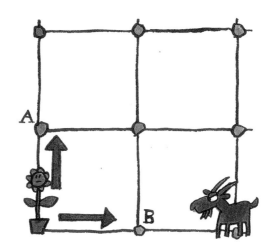

The flower can move one space to A or B (but moving to B would mean getting eaten).

This is how the goats can move:

The goat can eat flower X by jumping over it to A.
But it can't eat Y because that flower is protected by Z.

To win, the goats must eat all the flowers by jumping over them into empty spots.

The flowers win by surrounding the goats so they cannot move.

Will any of the gardener's flowers be saved? This depends on the skill and strategy used by the two players.

Lambs and Tigers

This is a strategy game like *Goats and Gardeners*. It is played by Hindu children in India.

Lambs and Tigers is a fight between two unequal forces.

There are fifteen lambs and only three tigers. But the tigers can move more freely and kill lambs by jumping over them. The lambs trap the tigers by surrounding them and stopping them from moving.

The players take turns placing pieces on the board and then moving them.

The lamb player must think:

'Where shall I move my lambs to trap the tigers?'

The tiger player also has to think:

'Which are the best positions for my pieces to catch the lambs?'

Thinking ahead like this is called strategy. Each player can plan his or her strategy and improve it every time they play.

Investigate games from around the world. How many strategy games can you find?

This strategy game is very popular in Sri Lanka with children. It is often played outside because the weather is warm.

These giant boards in the open air mean that lots of people can gather to watch as the players work out their strategies for *Draughts* and *Chess*.

Scrabble

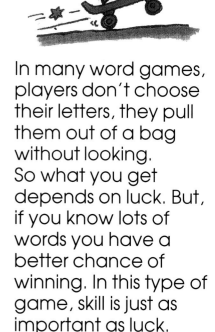

The word game in the picture below was made in Germany around 1860. It is called *The Alphabet Game* and was played by children to help them learn their spelling.

In many word games, players don't choose their letters, they pull them out of a bag without looking. So what you get depends on luck. But, if you know lots of words you have a better chance of winning. In this type of game, skill is just as important as luck.

Scrabble is a crossword game. Players score points by making words on a board out of letter tiles.

You can make and play a simple version of *Scrabble*. Start with a simple board with 15 by 15 squares (each 2 x 2cm) like this:

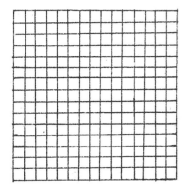

Then make 100 letter tiles, each 2 cm square. The list here shows how many of each letter of the alphabet you need. Use capital letters.

A 9	N 6
B 2	O 8
C 2	P 2
D 4	Q 1
E 12	R 6
F 2	S 4
G 3	T 6
H 2	U 4
I 9	V 2
J 1	W 2
K 1	X 1
L 4	Y 2
M 2	Z 1

Put all the tiles face down on the table and shuffle them around. Share them out amongst the players. It does not matter if you see each other's letters, so it helps if each player sets out their tiles in front of them.

The player with the letter 'X' goes first. The others take turns in a clockwise direction. There is no advantage in going first.

Each player takes it in turn to add a word to the board or complete a word. Words go:

horizontally:

or vertically:

New words must not touch other words.

It is a very good idea to have one person called the 'judge'. If there is an argument about spelling, the judge uses a dictionary to check the word.

The winner is either the first to use all his or her letter tiles, or, when no one can go, the player with the least tiles.

Notes for parents and teachers

Art, Crafts and Technology

• The playing boards can be painted on to thick card and stuck down on packaging cardboard. Protect the decorated boards with transparent plastic film. Children could sew and glue board games out of material to make fun wall-hangings. Giant boards could be painted on an old sheet or the squares for a race game could be made out of card and laid down in a large room.
• The playing pieces could be modelled from plasticine, or cut from card or balsa wood. You could buy them direct from model shops or use junk items such as bottle tops, buttons or yoghurt pots.
• Children can design and make up boxes to keep their board games safe in.
• They can compare and evaluate the materials used to make board games.

Drama and Physical Education

• Children can become the playing pieces and move around a giant board (see above).
• A team of six numbered children could be the die. A short race would determine the winner and thus the number of moves to be taken.

Maths

• Designing and drawing up boards involves planning and measuring. Scoring and using dice provides plenty of opportunity to practise counting, adding and other number skills.
• Playing games that are based on probability can make the concept easier to understand.
• Children could time a few rounds of a game and compare average times taken to play.
• They could cost the materials used in making their board games.
• Results of a survey of the most popular game could be presented as a bar graph or pie chart.

Language

• Children can read books and carry out research to find out about board games from around the world and their history. They can go on to write up the information they have found.
• Writing skills will also develop as they write out rules, explain strategies and make up names for the games. If they decide to market them, they can practise writing 'copy' for posters and advertisements, and make up a script for a commercial.
• Children will be able to listen and speak as groups take part in planning and designing games, explaining new games to other children and discussing ideas.

Geography

• Board games are played all over the world. This provides a good starting point for children to discover how other people live.
• Using a world map to pinpoint where games are played can help map-work skills.

History

• Children can compare today's board games with those played by people of their parents' and grandparents' age.
• They could research the origins and development of a particular board game and visit a museum that has a collection of board games.

Topic web

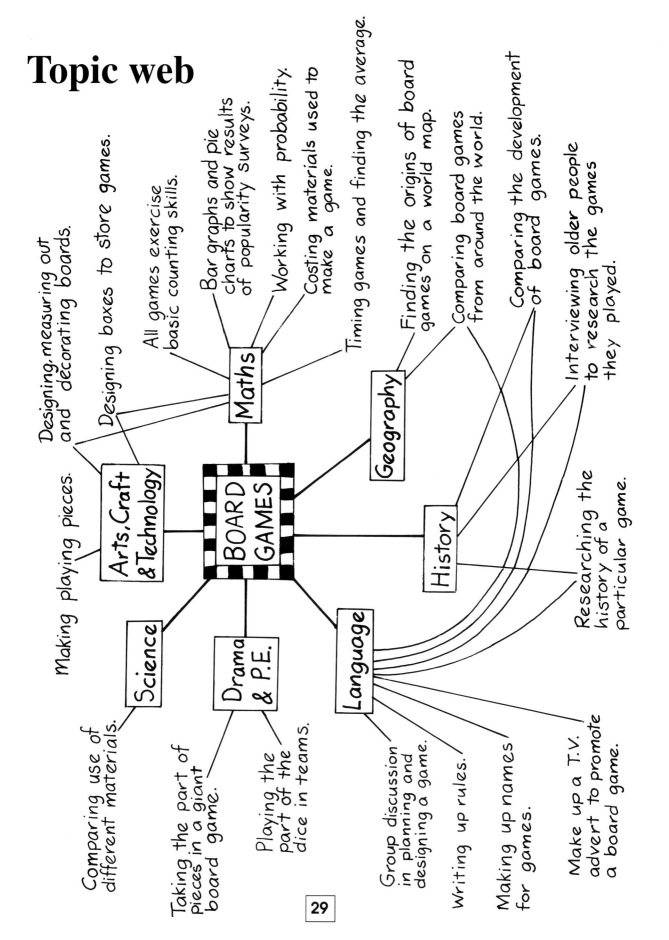

BOARD GAMES

Arts, Craft & Technology
- Designing, measuring out and decorating boards.
- Designing boxes to store games.
- Making playing pieces.

Maths
- All games exercise basic counting skills.
- Bar graphs and pie charts to show results of popularity surveys.
- Working with probability.
- Costing materials used to make a game.
- Timing games and finding the average.

Geography
- Finding the origins of board games on a world map.
- Comparing board games from around the world.

History
- Comparing the development of board games.
- Interviewing older people to research the games they played.
- Researching the history of a particular game.

Science
- Comparing use of different materials.

Drama & P.E.
- Taking the part of pieces in a giant board game.
- Playing the part of the dice in teams.

Language
- Group discussion in planning and designing a game.
- Writing up rules.
- Making up names for games.
- Make up a T.V. advert to promote a board game.

Glossary

Design   To plan how something will look and work. The plan or pattern for something.

Die   A square block with numbers on each face. Dice (more than one die) are used as decision makers in games.

Horizontal   Positioned on the board from left to right.

Petrol gauge   The dial that tells you how full the petrol tank is.

Probability   The chance that something will happen.

Skill   The cleverness that a player uses to play a game.

Strategy   The way a player plans and plays a game.

Vertical   Positioned from the top of a board to the bottom.

Picture Acknowledgements

The publishers would like to thank the following: The Board of Trustees of the Victoria and Albert Museum 18, 26; Chapel Studios 9, 19; David Cumming 25 top; Eye Ubiquitous 25 bottom; Wayland Picture Library (Zul Mukhida) *cover, title page;* ZEFA 15.

Finding Out More

There are very few books about board games published especially for children. But the books listed below can provide useful material for further investigations.

Board Games from Around the World. A pack of three large board games and a useful booklet of teacher's notes. Available from The OXFAM Youth and Education Department, 274 Banbury Road, Oxford. OX2 7DZ.

Board Games Round the World by R Bell and M Cornelius (Cambridge University Press, 1988). A resource book for mathematical investigations for 9-14 year-olds.

Games of the World (UNICEF, Zürich, 1982)

Gruesome Games – Twelve Great New Spine-Tingling Board Games by Shoo Rayner (Blackie, 1988)

Play the Game by Brian Love (Michael Joseph and Ebury Press, 1978). Although published a few years ago, this book provides very good explanations and full-colour illustrations of Victorian and Edwardian board games.

Toy and model museums are fun to visit. There are many to choose from, but the better-known ones include:

Bethnal Green Museum of Childhood
Cambridge Heath Road
London E2 9PA

Pollock's Toy Museum
1 Scala Street
London W1P 1LT

London Toy and Model Museum
21 Craven Hill
London W2 3EN

Museum of Childhood
Sudbury Hall, Sudbury
Derbyshire DE6 5HT

Index

32